Jacqueline Rose Farar

Word Gardening

Poems & Short Stories
to
Soothe the Soul

ISBN: 978-1-7328770-4-7.

Printed in the United States of America

All that is and can ever be lies in rich
abundance within yourself

—Jacqueline Rose Farar

To my family

CONTENTS

POEMS

SHORT STORIES

POEMS

NATURE'S VOICE

Gentle reader
Heed my words
Thoughts not formed
From a pondered mind
But gifted from an ancient oak,
Prophetic scrawl
From the great unknown.
Once discovered,
A rambling rose
Ventures down
Wakes the sleeping log
Alerts the wandering vine
Shares the message
With a passing breeze
Gathers cornered leaves
And circles a cloud
Around the earth.
Stilled in silence,
A wise owl speaks:
"A plague has spread across the planet
People fear the air they breathe

Friends and families, 'now risky strangers'
Microchips dictate the day.
Robotic lines in masked compliance
Emptied storefronts, shelves, and hope
Panic spikes in rising numbers
Human touch confined to screens.
Unchartered routes
Injecting promise,
Man lies victim to his fate."
The wise owl sighed.
"Fear not, beloved friends,
The inherent resiliency
Of man and nature
Is immune to ultimate disaster.
Each individual expression of being
Contributes to the colorful tapestry of life.
One strand pulled may disrupt the pattern
But can never destroy the essence of
What truly is."
Sadly, man's divine heritage
Has been distorted
And he misread nature's warning.
The inscription on the tree:
"Save the Planet"
Was prophesied for man,
Not us.

FAITH

When darkness clouds your Universe
With life's adhering pains
Showering thoughts of fears and doubts
Like cold prevailing rains
And you're left stranded in the storm
To evaluate the toll
It's time to raise the light of Truth
Umbrellaed in your soul.
For after every storm subsides
The sun will reappear
To kiss each rain-drenched flower
And evaporate the fear.
And strengthen those still standing tall
For they're the ones that know
In the aftermath of every storm
Is an opportunity to grow.

LITTLE CHILD

Little child, what's your future?
Do you even care to know?
Would you change or rearrange things?
Can't you let your feelings show?

You stare with vacant eyes that tell me,
Too much drugs and booze and pain.
You lived excitement for the moment,
But that thrill you can't sustain.

Last night he promised that he loved you,
You believed him and were lured,
Today, you know, you'll never see him,
Love is just another word.

You look so tired, standing before me,
Shoulders bowed in quiet despair.
You had to search for all the answers,
But couldn't find them anywhere.
I'd like to pick you up and hold you,
Gently wipe away your fears.

Yet, I find I only scold you,
I've made you shed so many tears.

Couldn't we try to come together?
Forgetting all that's been the past.
Let me help and understand you,
Renew a trust that's going to last.

You see, I recognize your problems,
For I was young once, just like you.
And my mother suffered with me,
Why she cried I never knew.

You have a lifetime waiting for you,
And it's important that you do.
For one day, standing before you,
Might be your little child, too.

CHANCE

Why is it necessary to take a chance?
To express yourself honestly
At the risk of losing a friend.
To love someone
Who might not feel the same.
To pursue a goal that's unrealistic
Only because you want it.
To seek you own answers
Instead of accepting what is told.
To live life to the fullest at whatever cost.

Because, perhaps by doing this,
You may discover who you really are—
By chance.

TRANSITION

Hospice nurse leaves room.
Relieved,
She opens her eyes.
No need to smile a lie.
Freedom breathes
Through her aloneness,
Filling the space between thoughts
With redefined clarity.
Boney fingers grip the sheets,
An eagle's claw on fallen snow.
A time bomb hanging overhead,
Dripping down the minutes.
Sagged cushion in a drab green chair
Crushed by the weight of a family's grief.
Thin light hems the curtain's edge,
At first, a ray of hope.
Like low tide swished along the shore,
Hushed whispering ebbs in and out,
Glazing into a multitude of shimmering faces,
Some more familiar than others,
But each one a ticketed passenger

On her journey through life.
For three days
They have gathered,
Silhouetted images
Expanding and contracting.
Silence looms,
The room curves into light.
Life and breath
Wed as one,
Resisting
Reconciling
Receding
Released.

NO GREATER LOVE

No greater love hath I than Thou
Exalted by Your power.
Your name I speak
Your truth I seek
To glorify each hour.
And yet, I know, You've told me so
Don't rise above another.
Your love profound
You claim is found
In the essence of each other.

IN THE SILENCE

In the silence you will find Him
All around you if you look
Smiling sweetly through the flowers
Rushing down a winding brook.
Splashing red on grand horizons
Footprints formed in grains of sand
Brushing leaves along a pathway
Gathered heaps, divinely planned.
Climbing up a garden wall
Stretched across an endless sea
Shoreline ripples rise and fall
Ribboned in translucency.
Wrapped around a giant trunk
Richly draped in velvet green
Pouring sunshine from above
Filtered through a foliage screen.
See the raven way up yonder
Drifting on an ocean sky.
In the distance, hear the thunder
Observe the tranquil butterfly.
Now pause… and listen to your breathing.

Allow the process to begin
For in the silence you will find Him
Waiting patiently within.

LIFE

Leaves
Fall softly
Spawning life
In fallowed seeds
Birthed in
Nature's labored breathing
Seeking light
Where tall grass grows.
Razored claws
That till the soil
Wing-tipped specks
In timbered wood.
Fallen trees
Sustain their hunger
Resurrected
In grained decay.
When clouds
Drop sheets
Of hammered rain
Filling ruts
Like streaming fingers

Hopscotched footprints
Wash into tiny ships
Of curled leaves
Sailing toward
A distant shore.
Treetops sway
With new resilience
Unifying
Earth and sky
A chorus blend
Of nature's presence
As all life-forms
Rejoice as ONE.

THE BEAUTY OF THE ORDINARY

A trampled gate
Invites me in
Pathways trespassing through open fields
Folded shadows on a creviced ledge,
I'm shepherded into nature's fold.
Shrub, chaparral, and sage
Vines that sleeve the prickly stem
The random spill of sun and rain,
A moment shared is full of grace.
With closed eyes
And awakened sight
I sense the presence of journeys past.
Heavy poles drag the ground
The icy blast of winter's breath
Black twigs crackling in an orange plume
Their imprint lingers in a different realm.
Moving toward a wooded glen
I find my place in the family tree
A fair-skinned birch, my confidant
Grassy clumps, my pillow.
Leaves drifting down

Like an afterthought.
Shadowed pansies hide their face
Golden nuggets in a grain of sand.
The exquisite beauty of the ordinary.

THE DEBATE

"What part of speech," the teacher asked,
"Does the word LOVE belong?
Now give some thought before you speak
To what is right or wrong."
A hand shot up, a voice cried out,
"A noun it has to be,
To love a person, place, or thing
That's what love means to me."
"Oh no, you're wrong, a verb it is,"
Another disagreed.
"To be in love is a state of being
This point, you must concede."
"You both are wrong," another chimed.
"Love is an adjective, for sure;
Love must describe the way you feel
In order to occur."
The class debated back and forth
Their arguments were heard,
The teacher glanced at the student in back
Who'd spoken not one word.
She hushed the room and called his name
And asked him for his view.

He seemed to gather up his thoughts
Before stating what he knew.
"You all are right," he softly said.
"These facts, we can't ignore;
Love is truly all you've said
But even so much more.
A smile, a touch, a perfect day
A moonlit night for two.
A helping hand, a laughing child
A friendship tried and true.
A thought, a voice, a prayer at night.
Is this not love, as well?
Love best defined is love expressed
Mere words are just a shell.
I guess the point I'm trying to make
Is to confine love is absurd,
For to acknowledge love in all that is
Is love itself, assured."
The young man's voice fell silent then
His message was complete
The debating class chose not to speak,
Acknowledging defeat.
All eyes and hearts were turned toward him
And in their smiles he knew
The love received for the love he gave
Had proved his viewpoint, true.

PREMONITIONS PROMPT ME TO PONDER

What lies out there beyond the stars
And calls my name through restless slumber
Forcing memories to erupt
From lifetimes buried long ago
Then prods me on to escape my ego
And seek the truth of who I am
And why I'm here
This belief I hold true
I am awareness
Unlimited
Unencumbered
Resonating in the essence of Divine Love
The embodiment of Oneness expressed
A stranger's laugh
The poet's muse
A child's sleeping face
Both the observer and the observed
I share in the fullness of all that is
And yet, forgetting my true identity
I am repeatedly tunneled back into a story I've birthed
Through the illusion of many lifetimes

Blindly seeking the perfection
I already am
The sequestered traveler
Navigating through tangled paths
Negotiating the relationships and events
That will translate the acts of love and betrayal
Into lessons on truth and understanding
Their stories woven into mine
A tight knot
Loosened through the tender strength
Of love and forgiveness
Doubt and fear
Disintegrated into fine dust of nothingness
By a simple act of kindness
Like the surrendered sigh
Of a withered rose
My eyes rest on the final chapter
GRATITUDE AND FORGIVENESS
But the journey does not end here
Sitting on the top of a grassy knoll
Wedged between the smooth grooves
Of a Banyan tree
A tattered image of
Brittle bones and blurred memories
I am ushered up beyond the hum
Of whirling branches

Past a shimmering audience
Of familiar faces
And released in glistening brilliance
Once again realizing
I am awareness
Unlimited
Resonating in the essence of Divine Love
Sharing in the fullness of all that is.

PRAYER

Dear Lord, Thou art mine
Hidden beneath the smallest leaf, Thee I find
Reflected up from crystal brooks
Woven words in sacred books
Each circumstance presents a sign
Thou art mine
Dear Lord, Thou art all
Fortressed in majestic pines, standing tall
Tumbling waves upon the sea
Stretched across the galaxy
Yet, answering the faintest call
Thou art all
Dear Lord, I am Thine
Precious gifts bestowed, the claim is mine
Bowing down on humbled knee
For You alone have set me free
I live in Thee, a love divine
For I am Thine

ALL ABOARD

Long train coming
Calls me to it
Thunders freedom, roars adventure.
Whistle blowing
Says to hurry
Time's a 'wasting
Why aren't you here?
Well, I'll tell you
I'm not ready
You've got your load
I've got mine.
Smokestack puffing
Wheels a 'grinding
The earth quakes beneath my feet
No use stopping
I'll just watch you
Snaking cross the countryside.
Seasons change now
So do people
Hopes are dimmed until you call

"You can do it, you can do it, you can do it, you
can do it, you can do it, you can do it"
Forever echoes in my ears.
Hear you screeching
Door slides open
Need some help getting up the steps
Children grown now
Memories failing
Take me with you
ALL ABOARD

THE AWAKENING

Life is just another dream
Amongst the countless others
Man unravels each life's scheme
By truths that he discovers.
When reality becomes that truth
Man then chooses to redeem
His love for God and all mankind
And awakes within the dream.

THE CLOTHESLINE

White sails curve into a balmy breeze
Wooden anchors precluding flight
Pinch tight.
And captured in the plight of billowed bluster
A child's face breathes in the sun and light.
Life, in its purest form lives here
A moment wrapped in sheer delight.
Small hands caress
The gentle movement
Against the silhouetted white.
Two legs slowly moving sideways
A mother's shape defines the space.
Childish daydreams collapse in baskets
Memories drift to a sacred place.

TEXAS ROUND-UP – THE GREAT DISCONNECT

The gate opened wide
Bulky heaviness girdled through.
Low moans rising
A thick cloud
Of kicked up dirt
Blurring fifty Longhorn cattle
Into a single mass
Of traumatized confusion.
Steel bars shut.
Single file
Wide-eyed terror
Silenced in the crashing thud
Of a cruel fate.
A bawling calf in an adjoining pen, trembles.

The door pulled open—
Eggs, milk, butter, pushed aside.
Wrapped paper
Slick pink
Unravels

Two grass fed,
Sterilized,
Sanitized,
Classified,
Top quality steaks.
Juicy chewiness
Promised in the bright red, marbled texture
Guaranteed in Prime USDA grading.
Savory tastiness materializes
In a memory.
A baby reaches
Through playpen slats
And whimpers.
Loving arms respond.

BUTTERFLY

Lovely butterfly on the sill
Sitting there so very still
A whispered breath, a shadow's trace
Bestow the essence of your grace.
Tho, textured in a filmy lace
Your fragile charm commands the space.
Translucent wings start to unfold
Revealing shades of brown and gold
Felt-tipped edges trimmed in black
Silken thread across your back.
Dusted velvet, they seem to be
Fanned in perfect harmony
As you move onward into flight
Flitting upward, left to right
I soon lose you from my sight
A tiny dot in a stream of light
A part of me is lifted too
Untethered, I am joined with you
And in the wake of that release
I find my own abiding peace.

WHAT DO YOU SEE?

When you awake each morning
And your thoughts are running free
And as you plan the day ahead
Tell me what you see.
A world full of chaos
Steeped in hostility
Or respect and understanding
For shared diversity.
A future filled with doubts and fear
All dreams drifting away
Or faith restored by gratitude
For what you have today.
Tell me what you see
Where there is hate, we seek forgiveness
Beyond the wars, we find peace
Behind dark clouds, rainbows shimmer
Love expands with its release.
The politician's angry rant
With no apology
While a gathering of sparrows
Play love songs just for me.

A thirsty earth cracks open
Volcanoes start to spew
Torrential rains flood farmlands
Tell us what to do.
Where there are problems, we seek solutions
Where there is need, we lend a hand
We do our part to help the planet
Firmly committed as ONE we stand
This is what we do.
Beyond the wars, we find peace
Behind dark clouds, rainbows shimmer
Love expands with its release.
Tell me what you see.

THE ANT

Today, as I lay in bed depressed
Too tired to think of getting dressed
From out of the corner of my eye,
I observed an ant passing by.
As he worked his way across my bed
I noticed, in his mouth, a piece of bread.
The bread, he carried, three times his size
And as I stared at him with admiring eyes.
He trudged along toward his destination
Showing no signs of aggravation.
What confidence he seemed to hold
Taking on such a heavy load.
I wondered would he reach his goal
Or would the stress finally take its toll?
I didn't wonder too much more
For the bread dropped suddenly to the floor.
He circled around, no hesitation
Then not showing any resignation
Climbed the covers down to the floor
To retrieve his loss or perhaps search for more.
A valuable lesson could not be denied

For no matter what happened, at least he had tried
And he didn't let obstacles that stood in his way
Prevent him from facing the rest of the day.
He shared a message that let me know
Gigantic truths, out of small things, grow
As I slipped on my robe, I heard myself say
I learned a lot from that ant, today.

LOVE IS ALIVE

It glitters through the trees
And warms the sparrow's nest.
It scatters leaves along the walk
And lends pearl drops of dew
To each new blade of grass.
It splatters light into nighttime blackness
And quenches the parched earth's thirsty soil.
It sits on the horizon in a dazzling ball
Of orange brilliance
And whispers songs through pine scent breezes.
It lingers in the eyes of young lovers
And in a mother's heart touched by a tiny hand.
It kisses the cheek of a weary wife
And follows an old man up a flight of stairs
Then greets him with smiling faces at the door.
It drops tears on a faded photograph
And flowers on an old tombstone.
It wraps an arm around a mourning friend.
It pets the panting dog's head
And shakes the enemy's hand.
Love waits patiently for those who can't forgive.

It's as fierce as a cornered feral
As sweet as a bleating lamb.
It is love
Resonating throughout all nature and all mankind.
Nothing more
Nor less.

RESPONSIBILITY

This is my life
I have chosen it.
I have worked hard to get to the place
I am now at.
I accept all responsibility for whatever
Mistakes have been made along the way.
I will not allow fear and guilt from
Those mistakes to overwhelm me
But use them as lessons to develop my
Spiritual growth.
Life's problems are just an illusion
For they are temporary and can only
Gain importance by my reaction to them.
I have learned that the ability to love
And forgive are the most difficult and
Important virtues to retain.
I remain steadfast in my beliefs
Optimistic in my hopes and
Determined in my goals
Whatever they may be.

MEDITATION

When we observe the world around us,
We experience meditation
In all God's creation.
The rise of the ocean moves toward shore differently
Than the sun and moon exchanging places
Or the flowers opening and closing their petals
But the flow of life force is as recognizable
As the Yogi breathing in and out.
When we accept this observation as truth
Our significance as being one with the Universe
Becomes all consuming
And the useless ego discards itself
Like the jumbled seaweed
Heaped along the shore.

THE TREE

Tell me, do you see the tree?
Swathed with floral majesty
An emerald crown of foliage green
Splattered gold spaced in between.
A billowed skirt with ruffled hem
Tiny buds on a slender limb
Leaves that dance on a breezy whim
Snips of blue, invited in.
Where twigs are spun, a sparrow's nest
Against a trunk, a stranger rests.
Ancient faces, a sacred ark
Shrouded in the rutted bark.
If you believe the tree is more
Than a leafy spine on the earthen floor
Then in your bond of unity
You'll feel the essence of the tree
And understand the truth you find
Comes from your heart and not your mind.

OBSERVATIONS FROM THE PARK

Passing nods and cordial smiles
Down nosed dogs in soft earth mounds
Wide arc showers on favored green
Scattered sparrows lift off.
Where shadows trace northern slopes
And tall grass bows to the passing breeze,
Soft weight of mulch, foliage, and shredded bark
Cushion me in a collage of crimson, cinnamon, and rust.
Emerald green reigns here.
Like a brown egg poised in an eagle's nest,
A pinecone drops onto a circled mound.
The subtle movement
Between air, branch, and earth,
Interchangeable, interactive, intangible.
The activity of nature, expressing itself,
Invites my participation.
I am both stilled and moved.
A brown dog barks from the adjoining hill,
Two crows argue over territorial rights
And a universe of crawling tininess
journeys past my bare feet

So small that the movement of the entire
Caravan does not disturb a blade of grass.

LIVING ROOMS

Shadows trace the open door
Spider veils in corners, snug.
Silence paused by a morning breeze
Gray-striped cat on a morning rug.
The sunlit touch on curtains drawn
Slips through the crease and slices the room.
Then settles on a crystal vase
Where opened yellow petals bloom.
A countertop with matching bowls
Two empty mugs, not put away.
A kitchen sill with sprouted herbs
A coffee pot to start the day.
Although no voice speaks for this room
Its essence dwell in those who see
And helps the poet find the words
That beautify simplicity.

THANKS FOR THE NEW DAY

Early in the morning
Before shadows slice terrace steps
And circle the orange tree
And tiny jasmine stars pinch the air with sweetness
And spindly movement tickles tall grass
Leaning against the breeze.
Before sunlight spreads through cinnamon branches
Like melted butter
And tilts the pansy's face
And curled leaves of golden brown
Cartwheel to piled corners.
Before black-winged clothespins line the wires above
And slick-tailed rodents tightrope walk across
While silhouetted honeysuckles define themselves
Hands, pressed together, lift in an altar or prayer.
Hands that hold a lifetime of stories
Hands that have smoothed the frayed fabric
Of pain and disappointment
And patched together pieces impossible to repair.
Sweet memories
And harsh lessons

Etched in the deep lines of fate
Carrying the consequences
Of hard labor and a loved one's touch.
Hands as open and trusting and forgiving
As the deeply rooted willow tree.
Whispering drifts through the dim light
And a small voice
Frail with age
But strong with conviction
Gives thanks for the new day.

MEDITATION AT SEA

I drift along the open sea
Destination unknown, unimportant.
To savor the serenity of this moment
Is all that's meaningful to me.
As far as the eye can see
There is nothing
But ocean and sky
In every shade of blue.
Gently rocked
By soothing waves
That cradle me
I am hushed back
Into the womb
Of nothingness and
In that nothingness
I become everything:
A misty stream
Radiating hues of blue and green
Silver and gold
I am the rhythm of the wave
The scent of the air

The smooth slide of warm sun.
My essence extends beyond
The scope of the human eye
Or understanding.
I am all that is
And it is good.
High above
A swarm of frenzied birds
Tear at each other
Jarring me back
Into the world of density.
Rules, restrictions
Crossroads and corners
Conflicts and confusion
Bumps and barriers
Freeways and fences
Legalities and loopholes
Soft flesh on a hard deck.
A fish drops from the sky
And slips beneath
The watery depths.
Not yet ready
To weigh in
I close my eyes
And drift some more.

REVELATION

Forever I've beseeched thee
In written words
In mighty sermons
In golden temples.
What miracles I've demanded
As proof of Your existence.
What disappointments have obscured
My outward search.
And now at last in the temple of silent wisdom
You arise in brilliant illumination
Spilling forth revelation after revelation
Allowing me to view in wondrous awe
Each buzzing bee
Each rising wave
Each soaring bird
Each splendorous sun
Pulsating in perfect rhythm with my own.
Truth has become simplicity
Simplicity has become magnanimous
And in recognition of my atonement with all creation
Comes the greatest truth of all
That You are not MY miracle
I am Yours.

REALIZATION

Every man must realize
Before his weary bones can rest
That the search for God's existence
Is the purpose of life's quest.
And when this realization
Is ready to be known
He'll awake in new perception
With the wonders being shown.
For every thought he'll have henceforth
And everything he'll see
Will be an astounding revelation
Of God's simplicity.
For every blade of grass that grows
Each creature of the sea
Even the gentle brook that flows
Shares His identity.
He'll shed all life's delusion
With insights so profound
Yet instead of mourning what he's lost
He'll rejoice in what he's found.
But why await that final day

To initiate this task
Because to bring God in your life
All you need to do is ask!

THE STORM

Ghost ships drifting on an ocean sky
Wisp into a funneled train
Gathered cotton candy puffs
Squeeze a droplet tear of rain.
Darkened hues seep through the fold
Shadows shelve a canyon wall
Leaves and pebbles swept along
Pulled into a blustered squall.
An orchestra of sound and movement
Willows bend and treetops sway
A feathered chorus of joyful singing
Daylight churns a milky gray.
Crackling streaks ignite the skyline
Thunder growls the lion's roar
The bloated sky, a bursting torrent
Slamming earth in its downpour.
Rivers flow above the crestline
Puddles fill and disappear
Yellow-slickered newsmen gather
Cars slide through a flood of fear.
Trees fall heavy onto rooftops

Trickles turn to waterfalls
Sandbags line diverted roadways,
Shouldering curbs like bulky shawls.
Children, dogs stare out car windows
Value packed with loving care
Bullhorns yelling out their warning
Told to go but don't know where.
Sirens wailing in the distance
Brake lights blurred through misted gray
A green frog languishes in the moment
Skims the water
And swims away

NATURE'S REALM

Within the seed a flower grows
Life's breath upon a bowed tree blows
Streams that form the pebbles round
Clouds that move without a sound
Shadows guiding day through night
Outstretched wings on upward flight
Mountains traced by morning sun
Petals closed when day is done
Magenta streaks in sunsets glow
Align with autumn leaves below
Nature's voice speaks quietly
Shrouded in life's mystery
Tho we treasure what we see
The message loud is "Simply Be."

ABOUT MAKING A POEM

The poem—
First spotted as a scarlet leaf
Scales down the thorny spine
Then morphs into a misty slide
Of early morning shine
Tall grass bowing to a passing breeze
Rousing rhythm from a feathered fern
Favored seashells on a windowsill
Cobwebs spun through a broken urn
Empty spaces, canyon walls
Full with reverence
Hidden places where groundhogs crawl
Untouched innocence
The weathered gate, a piece of art
Green mossy clumps, divine
Can words retrieve the heart's response
From moments left behind?
The poem finds me waiting
And gathers in my heart
The synchronized translation
Of language to impart

SHORT STORIES

THE CONNECTION

The tree sighed deeply, stirring the nestlings from the highest branches. Rumors whispered through a quickening breeze forewarned of a large cluster of pink-fleshed creatures due to brace the shores before nightfall—their intent to down the many generations of spruce, pine, and fir trees that had populated the valley since the sacred moon of new beginnings.

The elder pine extended his vision far beyond the valley, smiling momentarily at the seedlings produced the previous year; their slender trunks just now gaining strength to stand upright. He didn't dwell on how destroying the trees would devastate the balance and harmony of the surrounding elements: a prime source of nourishment, shelter, protection, and rejuvenation. Each tree was keenly aware of all life forms. Even the tiniest movement of a veiny leaf or the cracked emergence of new life was met with a celebration of rustled laughter. Yet, the tree knew his purpose in life was not to judge, but "to be."

A spotted fawn and its mother stopped at the base of the tree, nibbling on the tender grass growing between its roots. Their ears rotated forward, alerting them to any sounds of impending danger. On an adjoining hill, a bristle-coated black bear stood backside against a tree, his throaty growl punctuating the back and forth movement. Tiny insects danced around his massive head, lifting and settling with each stroke. A struggling rodent caught in the grasp of a red-tailed hawk was carried and dropped into a treetop nest, where tiny mouths opened wide, anticipating its arrival.

That night, gathering clouds blanketed a shy moon. Growing apprehension swelling up from beneath the earth had prompted many of the burrowed groundhogs, rabbits, and foxes to spend the night scurrying from snarled bushes to hollow logs for safety. Even the nighttime predators refrained from taking easy prey, instead repeatedly circling the perimeter of their territory, sniffing the air for some sort of explanation. Total blackness eventually cloaked its heavy weight, and except for the mournful wail of the gray wolves, the forest was eerily quiet.

The morning sky was an angry black and crimson. Flames swept through the meadow and devoured a hillside of the mountain terrain. Animals ran panicked in all directions, undaunted by the huge trucks rushing past them. A convoy of helicopters maneuvered their way through the mountain pass, dropping water from a nearby lake. Orders were being shouted from all directions.

Fire departments were called in from several counties, and within two days it was over. Amongst themselves, the loggers blamed each other. The campfire wasn't properly extinguished. Joe didn't stamp out his cigarette. Earl probably ignited a spark testing the equipment. By the time the news hit the airwaves, a top heavy, mini-skirted weather girl looked straight into the camera and blamed it on a lightning strike.

The elder tree stood unscathed but an entire hillside had been reduced to charcoaled skeletons—their stunted limbs raised in brute protest of man's assault against nature. For weeks, smoke-choked air consumed the atmosphere, and it wasn't until a year later before tiny sprouts reappeared.

A hundred miles away, six-year-old Claire sat on the porch, peering into a plastic pot. "I'm sure it's either a spruce or a fir tree," her grandmother commented. "Look, it's still healthy." She stroked the spiny trunk. "And see, there's even new growth on the branches. Feel for yourself." Claire gently touched the rough edges of the foot-high plant, then pulled back. It seemed so fragile. Sensing Claire's apprehension, the grandmother stated, "These guys are pretty darn strong. You know, people say the wind can blow a seed a thousand miles away, and that tiny seed, without help from anyone, can grow into a gigantic tree so tall, you can't even see the top." She stretched out her arms and lifted her head back to emphasize her point. "This big, I swear." Claire's eyes widened. "Well maybe not a thousand miles," her grandmother laughed. "But at least a hundred."

Claire pictured a seed flying along the freeway, over rooftops, between office buildings, past the schoolyard playground, and settling in a backyard where it grew taller than a giant beanstalk. She pictured herself swinging from one of its giant limbs or spying on people below from a secret spot hidden in the branches. Silently reviewing all the possibilities, she turned the pot around, trying to decide which side should face forward once it was planted.

Claire's grandmother smiled, clasping her hands together. "I just knew you would love it. The lady at the garage sale gave it to me for free. Just like that, she said, 'You take it. It's yours.' Said she was replacing her whole yard with gravel because of the drought. And that's not all," her grandmother added, exuding the enthusiasm of a made-for-TV kitchenware commercial. Pulling a coloring book from a large canvas bag, she quickly flipped through the pages in front of Claire's face. "Look, more than half the pages haven't even been colored on." And then one by one, a treasure chest of unwanted items was lifted from the bag: a doll with a missing leg, "You can pretend you're a nurse"; a pink rhinestone dog collar twirled around her finger, "You never know and a ball of yellow yarn. Claire's grandmother slowly shook her head, "Hmm, hmm, hmm, the possibilities are endless with this one."

Claire considered each new item, but her heart and thoughts were transfixed on the little plant, envisioning the giant tree it would one day become.

THE TRAIN

Her earliest memory of the passing train was of her running across an open field to wave to the conductor. She always arrived early, leaning across the embankment, watching for the curled column of thick black smoke rising beyond the bend, listening for the whistle blowing above the strain of grinding wheels. Waving wildly in its direction, she imagined herself as one of the faces looking out the window, scanning the faraway places she had only seen in picture books.

Over the years, her sense of wonderment was dimmed by hardship and tragedy. It flashed red across the driveway, hung in the silence of a dropped phone, grieved in the doorway of an emptied room. Chaos and conflict blew through like a Texas tornado, but the train's reverberating roar calmed her into replaying memories of being a little girl, running across the field, feeling a child's joy.

Only now, the tall grass she had once rushed through was buried beneath tract houses, broken sidewalks, gutted streets, old cars, and dumpsters. She could only catch a glimpse of the train as it moved between houses like sliding doors.

With her family grown and scattered elsewhere, she would often take the bus to the train station and sit on the platform. Age and economics had bridled her spirit, but each time the train screeched to a stop, she breathed an exhilarating sigh, like anxiously awaiting a beloved friend.

Up close, the train was an imposing presence of polished grittiness, but her favorite memories were when it was a long black snake, calling to her from the distance, repeating the same message it had chanted to her throughout her life: "You can do it, you can do it, you can do it, you can do it, you can do it, you can do it, you can do it, you can do it, you can do it," echoing forever in her ears.

PERCEPTION

I stare into the empty cup and wonder whether or not to pour one more cup of coffee. What I'd really like to do is look inside and see my future, like that old fortune teller did with the tea leaves at the county fair. Said I'd be rich by the time I'm twenty-one. That's a laugh!

I'd like to see her now and show her my shoes with holes worn clear through, or maybe impress her with my dress and matching curtains. I could even invite her to this dump to see how the rich really live.

I look down at hands that are calloused and worn from chopping wood, tending kids, and scrubbing floors—that reek of ammonia and sometimes dirty diapers. Yeah, I've been blown up and deflated three times now. The youngest is only six months and he's the worst of the lot. As fast as I can shove food in one hole, it comes out the other. And sometimes when he's got both ends going at once, I join right in and cry along with him… 'cuz I know it's just a waste. My pamperin' and powderin' that soft pink skin so someday he can be like his daddy, comin' back from the mines, dirty and black with that same hacking cough.

Yeah, that daddy of his'll come home tonight, all bent over, put his lunch pail on the counter and peek inside the kettle like we was having somethin' different than those same black beans. And he'll sit down at the table, grinnin' like a fool, kids crawling all over him like nursin' puppies. It'll be a night no different than the others. His talkin' about what happened at the mine to no one listenin'. And if he tells a joke, he'll laugh so hard, it'll make me hate him 'cuz he's not even funny… or handsome… or smart. He's just there.

I push my body away from the table and drag it down the hall toward the bedroom. Might as well make the beds this morning so we can mess 'em up tonight. A vacuum cleaner blocks my path, reminding me not to neglect the floors. I remembered how joyed I was to get it for my anniversary two years ago. We only got three payments left and it'll be mine for real.

A neighbor knocks on the door and asks if she can borrow my anniversary present 'cuz hers is out of bags. So I tell her, "Sure, and don't bother returning it for at least a year." And she looks at me sideways and asks if I'm feeling poorly, and tho I'm wishing I was dead, I tell, "No, I'm feeling just fine, thank you." But she just keeps talkin' and talkin' about everyday nothin' till the words start makin' about as much sense as a chained dog, barkin'. I finally just push the vacuum through the door, and close it. And she stands there and keeps barkin' till she finally gets tired and leaves.

So now, after lookin' around at what has to be done, I just crawl into bed and pull the covers up over my head, shutting out everything around me.

And that's when those big 'ol crocodile tears start comin' so fast my whole body shakes. If my momma was still alive, she'd be tellin' me, "Go ahead Louella, and wallow in that self-pity till you can't wallow no more." Well, that's exactly what I intend to do: wallow till I'm lower than a pig in slop and if I can go lower than that, I'll do it.

Pretty soon I'm bawlin' worse than a newborn calf, and that damn kid of mine starts cryin' 'cuz one of those holes needs tendin' to. And here we go again, cryin' together. His pain callin' me to him and my pain beggin' to be left alone.

Next thing I know, the phone's ringin' and I'm wailin' at the top of my lungs, "Mama, please help me. Tomorrow, I'm gonna be twenty-one and my life's done over with."

"Is this Mrs. Cooley? Mrs. Louella Mae Cooley?" a voice asks.

I immediately sit upright, flinging the covers away. If my middle name's being mentioned in a conversation, it must be important.

"Yes, it is," I answer, my heart poundin', full of fear.

"Congratulations, Mrs. Cooley, you are the Grand Prize winner of the Mercantile County Fair lottery. A ticket worth twenty-five thousand dollars. I just need to ask you a few questions, and then I hope you can get down here right away. The reporters are already on their way."

At first, I think I must be dreaming, but no, I did play the lottery that day at the fair. And the guilt just about killed me for spending money so foolishly. And those hungry little faces starin' up at me were constant reminders of my stupidity.

Then it hits me: Twenty-five thousand dollars! I can barely write down the information, I'm so excited. The whole time I'm in the shower, I feel like singin' my fool head off, but all I can do is think about how Charlie's gonna look at that empty kettle tonight with disappointment till he smells that turkey with all the trimmings hidden in the oven. And before he can even ask why I'm wearing my special occasion dress… or why the kids are all lined up, faces scrubbed shiny as a new penny, I'll show him the check… and we'll be laughin' and huggin' and squealing like pigs in slop.

I think I got the money half spent even before I get dried off, and as I grab up that sleepin' bundle of love and rush out the door, the last thing I see is that little brown teacup… just starin' at me.

NATURE'S GIFT

Morning mist lifting. Wide-winged ravens circle low. A splattered rainbow of wildflowers spills everywhere. Awakened movement in treetop's sway. Incredulous beauty surrounds me, yet my thoughts follow the weeded pathway obscured in tall grass. Its directionless meandering metaphorically projects the uncertainty of my own life.

Several feet away, a blue jay tweezes tiny insects from a rotted log. He stretches one spindly leg and fans out into multi-shades of blue. Swiping his beak from side to side, he extricates more insects, then hops further down the log to gather more food. I watch with both envy and admiration. "If my life were only as simple as yours," I muse.

As if reading my thoughts, the blue jay turns in my direction. "Why, you look pretty contented right now. What's wrong with this moment?" I stare dumbfounded. This has to be my imagination. A bird can't really be talking to me. I swear, he stares at me straight in the eye. "Well?" he probes.

In spite of the absurdity of the situation, I feel compelled to respond to his voice in my head.

"Oh, this moment is fine. It's all the other moments in my life that are giving me problems."

The blue jay cocks his ruffled head. "Hmm, that's a strange thought. Think about it. Isn't this the only moment that actually exists?" And before I can even digest his opinion or argue my own, he flies off. A tiny spot, high in the sky.

I have to walk. I have to think. What just happened couldn't have really happened. I mean everyone knows birds don't talk to humans. Unless their parrots. There's obviously too much stress in my life. Somehow things that just don't make sense are making sense in a crazy, delusional way.

I haven't taken more than a couple of steps before a raspy voice stops me dead in my tracks. "Pay less attention to the messenger and more to the message," it demands.

Right in the middle of the path, lies a humongous beetle on his back, legs flailing in the air. "And would you be so kind as to help turn me over so I can be on my way. I've been stuck like this all morning, just waiting for you."

My mind helplessly responds to this impossible charade, "But how did you even know I'd even be here? I mean, someone else could've walked by and squished you without giving it a second thought."

"Haven't you learned anything about what was said to you about living in the moment? Besides, I volunteered to be here. We knew you would probably need a second opinion. Your type, always doubtful."

"The only thing I'm doubting IN THIS MOMENT is my sanity," I snap.

"NOW, please," he moans.

"Oh yes, I'm sorry I forgot about your predicament." The beetle quickly grasps the extended twig I offered and disappears into the brush. But not without first raising his butt with indignation at my obvious lack of awareness.

Piled leaves curl in laughter.

My attention turns to a distant grove of fair-skinned birch trees. A strengthening breeze twirls past me and partners with the long-legged beauties. Dancing wildly, slender limbs lifted, they sway together in complete abandonment. Wind and trees join in unison, quickly escalating into one magnificent spiral of energy.

I am drawn toward one particular tree that has been "graffitied" with scrawled initials embedded in its trunk. As I soothe the scarred bark, it interrupts my thoughts. "Please don't misjudge the essence of what I am by the thoughtless actions of others. This is important for you to remember. Their story is not who I am. Nor is your story, you."

Overwhelmed, I cannot digest all this newfound information nor the source from which it is given. The tree understands. "Follow the slope beyond the third rock grouping; there is a narrow stream. Sit quietly and listen. Free-flowing water always brings the best clarity."

Instinctively guided, I am soon resting near a bend in the stream. Frothy water bubbles around smooth rocks and broken twigs. An indefinable transformation takes place and I fold into a blur of colors, textures, movement, and sensations. Reality is redefined beyond my ability to understand or clarify.

Sunlight rests on a heavy boulder anchored deep beneath the water's surface. Grassy strands fringe the water's crest like a circled skirt. "Did you know I used to be bigger than that pine tree behind you?" it asks.

At this point, I can only shake my head. "Well, it's true," it adds. "Over the eons, I've been every shape, size, and color imaginable. Been sat on, spat on, slept on, played on, prayed on, cried on, died on, straddled, rattled, ritualized, crystalized, idolized, symbolized, tossed, crossed, and mossed… like you see me now."

With the rhythm of a shoreline wave, a misty spray intermingles with the mossy strands. No response could match the magnitude of what the rock had just revealed. He respects my moment of reflection and continues speaking.

"Well, the point I'm trying to make is this: Regardless of whatever circumstance or form I take, the 'I' of me remains unchanged. I am not affected by past, present, or future situations because I exist only in this moment. This truth, you know also."

Overcome with emotion, an overflow of dreamlike memories dissipates into nothingness. Immersed in the sacred connectedness of all life—time, circumstance, and restrictions no longer exist. Only love.

Savoring the awareness of each step, I slowly climb up over the embankment. A green frog skitters past. "Hope to see you at the frog concert tonight. It starts at dusk."

I look in both directions. On one side, shadows puddle in dark crevices, leading deep into the forest. On the other side, sunlight smiles wide in open meadows. It doesn't matter which path I take. They're all good.

ABOUT THE AUTHOR

Jacqueline Rose Farar is a retired Social Worker, living in Granada Hills, California. Most of her adult life has been dedicated to working with the homeless population, abused children, and persons with developmental disabilities and traumatic head injuries. Jacqueline has also volunteered at various hospitals and rehabilitation facilities teaching dance therapy, as well as conducting meditation classes for young adults with cancer. She is the mother of four children, four grandchildren, and two great grandchildren. She is a lover of nature, poetry, and all things beautiful.

Made in the USA
Monee, IL
10 May 2021

67163029R00049